TUDOR	STU		VICTORIAN	MODERN TIMES
1485-1603	1603		1837-1901	1902-NOW

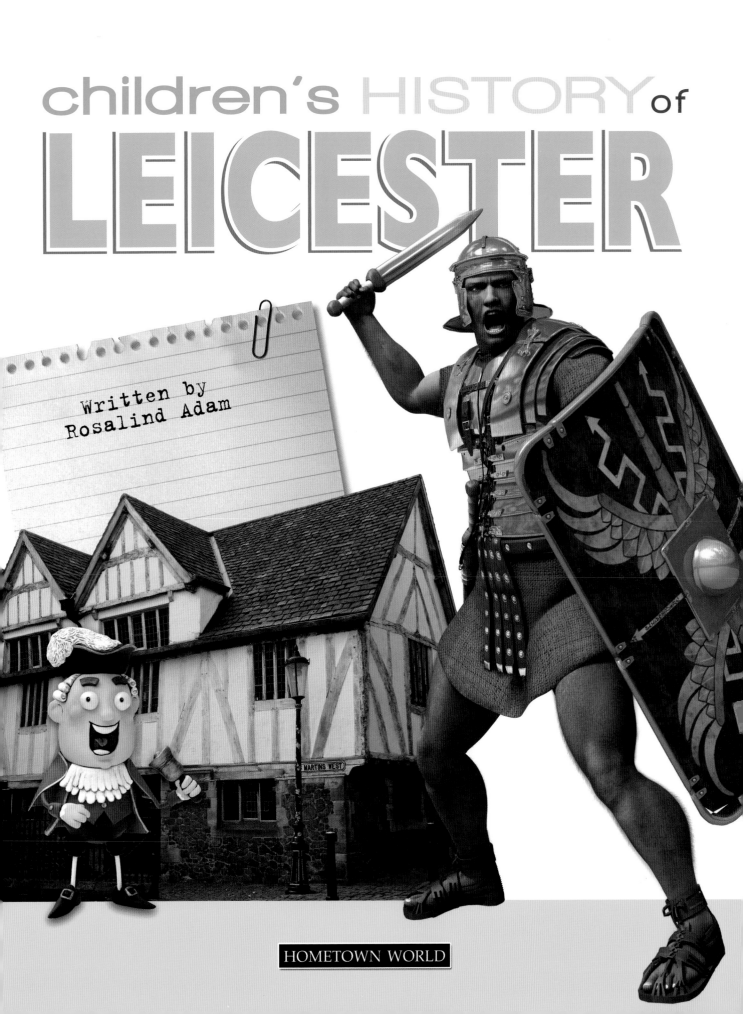

children's HISTORY of
LEICESTER

Written by
Rosalind Adam

MARTINS WEST

HOMETOWN WORLD

How well do you know your town?

Have you ever wondered what it would have been like living in Leicester when the Romans arrived? What about working as a stocking weaver instead of going to school? This book will uncover the important and exciting things that happened in your town.

Want to hear the other good bits? You will love this book! Some rather brainy folk have worked on it to make sure it's fun and informative. So what are you waiting for? Peel back the pages and be amazed at what happened in your town.

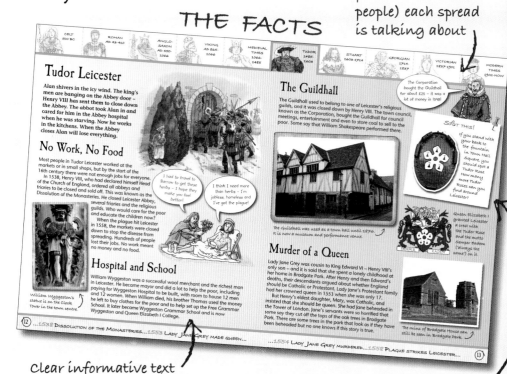

Timeline shows which period (dates and people) each spread is talking about

Clear informative text

'Spot this!' game with hints on something to find in your town

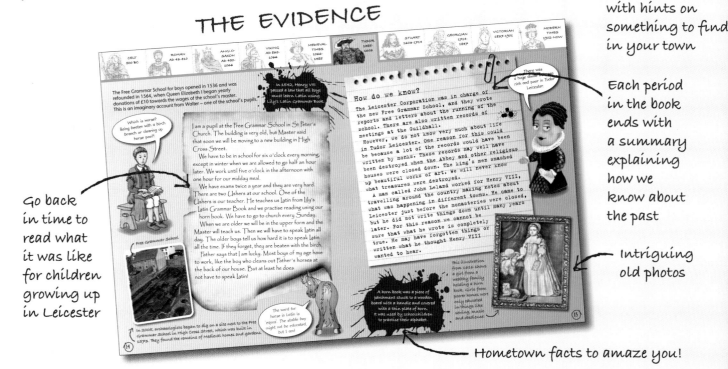

Go back in time to read what it was like for children growing up in Leicester

Each period in the book ends with a summary explaining how we know about the past

Intriguing old photos

Hometown facts to amaze you!

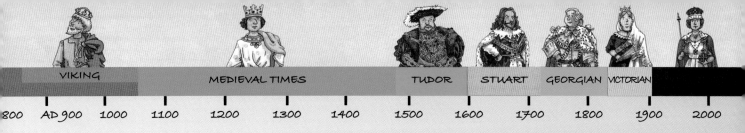

Contents

CELT
500 BC

ROMAN
AD 43-410

ANGLO-SAXON
AD 450-1066

VIKING
AD 865-1066

MEDIE
TIME
106
148

Ratae Corieltauvorum

Primus stands in the doorway to the atrium. It's his first day as a slave at the big house and he doesn't want to upset his new master, who has just arrived from Rome with his family. Primus's hands are trembling so much that the glass wine cups on the tray he's holding start to rock and rattle. The master's wife turns and spots him – and he trembles even harder. Thankfully, the master and his daughter, Livia, are too busy to notice him. His master is scowling at the rain outside and Livia is gazing at the beautiful mosaic floor.

Mosaic pavements were made up of thousands of tiny pieces of tile. Making them was painstaking work.

The Roman Invasion

The Romans invaded Britain in AD 43, gradually moving north and taking over the lands of Celtic tribes – sometimes peacefully and sometimes after fierce battles. The Romans marched into the area that is now Leicester by AD 47, looking for somewhere to cross the River Soar without sinking into mud, and the local Corieltauvi tribe could not stop them.

The Romans built a fort to protect their river crossing. In the town, they made roads in a neat grid and put up lots of impressive buildings, including a large bathhouse. They built the long, straight Fosse Way and turned the town into an important civitas, which means it was like a capital city. The Romans called this place Ratae Corieltauvorum.

The Fosse Way runs from Exeter to Lincoln, via Leicester. Parts of the Fosse Way are still busy roads today – the Romans would have been proud.

My knees are red raw and I've been working since dawn. The master better be pleased!

He's never pleased! However beautiful the mosaics are, he always thinks they could be better.

SPOT THIS!

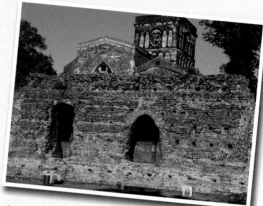

The Romans built rows of hard, red brick into the walls of their bathhouse so that it would last a long time. It's lasted nearly 2,000 years so far! You can take a closer look at the walls at the Jewry Wall Museum.

Roman Ways

The Roman soldiers lived in Ratae Corieltauvorum for just 30 years. When the soldiers were ordered to march north, many Romans stayed. By now, people from the Corieltauvi tribe lived like Romans, too, and the town prospered.

Leicester has always been known for its markets. The Romans called it the forum – an open courtyard with a market and rows of shops. The forum was somewhere beneath where the busy St Nicholas Circle is now. Nearby was the Roman bathhouse. The baths were not just for washing. The Romans met friends and had business meetings there, too. Some lived in large town houses beautifully decorated with mosaics and wall paintings. One of Leicester's houses had a mosaic pavement with a peacock at the centre – it must have belonged to a very rich family.

The Romans loved to eat roast peacock.

This fragment of painted ceiling plaster was once part of Leicester's Roman market hall, or Macellum.

CELT
500 BC

ROMAN
AD 43-410

ANGLO-
SAXON
AD 450-
1066

VIKING
AD 865-
1066

MEDI
TIM
106
148

Leicester's Roman baths had cold, warm and hot rooms – plus an excercise room where visitors could keep fit and play games. Here, a young slave boy called Amicus talks about his day working at the baths.

My worst job is using the strigil – it's a tool for scraping dead skin and oil off someone's body. Yuck!

I am the youngest slave at Ratae's baths. I will be 10 years old next month. When I first started work, I used to get lost as there are so many different baths and rooms all full of slabs where people lie to have their bodies massaged with sweet smelling oils.

Every morning I have to tend to the furnaces that heat the water and warm the rooms. It's sweaty work, so I'm glad to begin my next job – selling oysters to the bathers in the cold room. Next I take them to the warm room, and then finally the hot rooms. This is where I sell the most. People sit and talk in the hot baths and steam rooms. Some people talk about work. Some gamble with dice or knucklebones. They certainly all like to eat oysters!

Later today, something very exciting is happening. A famous gladiator called Lucius is coming for a bath and a massage. The older slaves won't let me serve him, but I'm hoping I might get to carry his clothes and oils. Lucius is in love with the actress Verecunda – everybody knows it!

We are serving drinks in the special glass cups that have the gladiators' names on them. This will make Lucius happy, and then maybe he will come and visit the baths again. Maybe he will bring Verecunda next time?!

This Roman glass cup is decorated with the figures of gladiators. It even shows their names around the top.

All Romans go to the baths – from emperors to farmers. Only slaves are forbidden!

TUDOR
1485-1603

STUART
1603-1714

GEORGIAN
1714-1837

VICTORIAN
1837-1901

MODERN TIMES
1902-NOW

The Romans laid the foundations for Leicester, and it quickly grew into a busy market town.

This piece of pottery has the inscription, 'Verecunda the actress and Lucius the gladiator'.

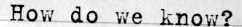

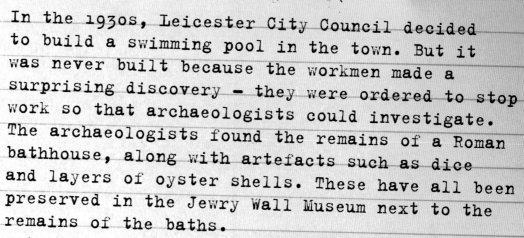

How do we know?

In the 1930s, Leicester City Council decided to build a swimming pool in the town. But it was never built because the workmen made a surprising discovery — they were ordered to stop work so that archaeologists could investigate. The archaeologists found the remains of a Roman bathhouse, along with artefacts such as dice and layers of oyster shells. These have all been preserved in the Jewry Wall Museum next to the remains of the baths.

Archaeologists have also found other evidence to show that Leicester was an important town in Roman times. The remains of mosaics and wall paintings were discovered, which tells us that there were town houses belonging to rich people. In a lucky twist of fate, a painted wall had fallen onto a mosaic floor and each had kept the other from being worn away.

Lots of small pieces of Roman pottery, glass, coins and even a lead curse tablet have been dug up over the years. The oldest Roman coin ever found in Britain was dug up in Hallaton, just outside Leicester. Each piece we find tells us a little about life in Roman times.

This lead tablet has a curse on it written in Latin. It asks the God Maglus to kill a thief who had stolen a coat from a man called Servandus.

7

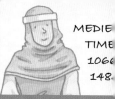
Saxons and Danes

Hilda is preparing supper while her mother rounds up the geese to sell at market. Hilda is Anglo-Saxon. She dare not go far from home because the Vikings might hurt her. Suddenly she hears horses' hooves, spears clashing and people shouting. Queen Ethelfleda has brought her army to drive the Vikings away! Hilda shouts to her mother to come home, then dashes inside for cover.

Historians have reconstructed Anglo-Saxon buildings on their old foundations – it really helps us to imagine how they lived.

The Anglo-Saxons

By the start of the 5th century AD, the Roman army had gone and the people of Ratae were left to fend for themselves. Before long, the houses and public buildings of the Roman city began to fall into ruin. At about this time, Anglo-Saxon settlers arrived from Europe and built timber halls and huts among the Roman ruins. One hut was built right on top of the collapsed wall of a massive Roman market hall.

Christianity Comes

In AD 653, the son of Penda the King of Mercia became a Christian and by the 670s Leicester had its own bishop. Some think Leicester's first cathedral was St Nicholas Church, which was built against the Roman Jewry Wall. Others think it was St Mary de Castro or St Margaret's. All three still stand today. If only they could talk!

Parts of St Nicholas Church date from Saxon times. There is even evidence of Roman building work. →

...AD 450 ANGLO-SAXONS COME TO LEICESTER...AD 653 CHRISTIANITY ARRIVES

Viking Invasion

In AD 877, another army of invaders and settlers arrived. These were Vikings, or Danes, from Scandinavia. They took over much of northern and eastern England – an area known as the Danelaw. The Vikings invaded and made Leicester one of their important Five Boroughs.

Anglo-Saxon King Alfred, however, was determined to defend England against the Vikings. His daughter, Ethelfleda, recaptured Leicester and strengthened the walls around the town to keep the Danes out.

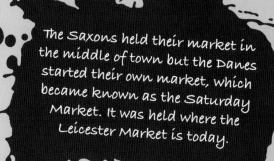

The Saxons held their market in the middle of town but the Danes started their own market, which became known as the Saturday Market. It was held where the Leicester Market is today.

How do we know?

In 1866, the skeleton of an Anglo-Saxon lady was found in Glen Parva on the outskirts of Leicester. Known as the Glen Parva Lady, she had been buried with her jewellery, a glass beaker and two bone plates that are thought to have been knife handles. These things tell us a little bit about how she and other Anglo-Saxons in this area lived.

The Anglo-Saxon Chronicle was an important diary that King Alfred ordered his men to write in the 9th century AD. It was still being updated until the 12th century, and has given us lots of important information. For example, without it we would never have known about Ethelfleda and her battle with the Vikings in Leicester.

SPOT THIS!

The Glen Parva Lady's skeleton is on display in the Jewry Wall Museum. There is also a reconstruction to show how she may have looked when she was alive.

This was the Dark Ages for Leicester – a time still shrouded in mystery.

CELT
500 BC

ROMAN
AD 43-410

ANGLO-
SAXON
AD 450-
1066

VIKING
AD 865-
1066

MEDIEV
TIME
1066-1

The Earl's Town

The air smells of hot bread. William has been sent to collect a tray of his father's loaves from one of Leicester's bread ovens. The Earl of Leicester owns all the ovens, so William has to pay to have the loaves baked. When he walks home through the market, the earl's men will be collecting money from the market traders. The earl owns the market, too. He's a rich and powerful man, but most people in the town are poor.

Phew, it's hot in here – they don't call this Bakehouse Lane for nothing!

William the Conqueror ordered the building of Leicester Castle. It was a motte and bailey castle, and the mound can still be seen in Castle Gardens.

The Abbey was destroyed by fire in 1645, but the ruins can still be seen today in Abbey Park.

The Earls of Leicester

William the Conqueror was King of England from 1066 to 1087. He appointed earls to rule over Leicester. As they were close to the king, Leicester often had royal visitors.

Around 1143, Earl Robert de Beaumont founded Leicester Abbey. One of the abbots, Henry Knighton, kept a diary so we know a little about life in the Abbey. Henry, Earl of Lancaster and Leicester, added the Newarke in about 1330 (which used to be called New Work) and the grand Magazine Gateway.

Probably Leicester's most famous earl, Simon de Montfort, was responsible for the first English parliament in 1265, with elected members from different counties. One of Leicester's universities and a concert hall are named after him.

TUDOR
1485-1603

STUART
1603-1714

GEORGIAN
1714-1837

VICTORIAN
1837-1901

MODERN
TIMES
1902-
NOW

The Parliament of Bats

While the earls, barons and lords fought, Leicester Abbey grew rich and powerful.

Parliament sometimes met in Leicester. After some of the barons attending had a row, everyone was forbidden from bringing weapons into the Great Hall in case they started to fight. They hid clubs, or 'bats', under their clothes. This gathering in 1426 became known as the Parliament of Bats.

Legend says that Richard's head struck Bow Bridge as his body was carried off the battlefield on horseback.

Last Medieval King

In the mid 1450s, England went to war as two noble families – the House of York and the House of Lancaster – battled for power. Yorkist Richard III fought under a white rose emblem and the Lancastrians fought under a red rose. It became known as the Wars of the Roses.

On 21st August, 1485, Richard fought Henry at the Battle of Bosworth Field, 19 km west of Leicester. Richard was killed. Henry displayed his body in the Newarke for three days to prove he was dead, and was then crowned Henry VII – the first Tudor king.

Nell was a serving girl at the White Boar Inn in Leicester. This is her account of what took place on the day of King Richard III's death.

I had prepared breakfast for the king and now I watched him set off with his army. As he rode across Bow Bridge, his foot knocked against the cornerstone. An old lady, called the Witch of Daneshill, was watching. I was afraid of her. "When next he comes over that bridge," said the old lady, "it will be his head that knocks the cornerstone." Later that day her words came true.

SPOT THIS!

Bow Bridge is worth a closer look. See if you can spot this stone head or one of the plaques that tells the story of Richard III's death.

11

CELT
500 BC

ROMAN
AD 43-410

ANGLO-
SAXON
AD 450-
1066

VIKING
AD 865-
1066

MEDIE
TIM
106
148

Tudor Leicester

Alan shivers in the icy wind. The king's men are banging on the Abbey door – Henry VIII has sent them to close down the Abbey. The abbot took Alan in and cared for him in the Abbey hospital when he was starving. Now he works in the kitchens. When the Abbey closes Alan will lose everything.

No Work, No Food

Most people in Tudor Leicester worked at the markets or in small shops, but by the start of the 16th century there were not enough jobs for everyone.

In 1538, Henry VIII, who had declared himself Head of the Church of England, ordered all abbeys and friaries to be closed and sold off. This was known as the Dissolution of the Monasteries. He closed Leicester Abbey, several friaries and the religious guilds. Who would care for the poor and educate the children now?

When the plague hit Leicester in 1558, the markets were closed down to stop the disease from spreading. Hundreds of people lost their jobs. No work meant no money and no food.

I had to travel to Barrow to get these herbs – I hope they make you feel better!

I think I need more than herbs – I'm jobless, homeless and I've got the plague!

William Wyggeston's statue is on the Clock Tower in the town centre.

Hospital and School

William Wyggeston was a successful wool merchant and the richest man in Leicester. He became mayor and did a lot to help the poor, including paying for Wyggeston Hospital to be built, with room to house 12 men and 12 women. When William died, his brother Thomas used the money he left to buy clothes for the poor and to help set up the Free Grammar School. It later became Wyggeston Grammar School and is now Wyggeston and Queen Elizabeth I College.

TUDOR
1485-
1603

STUART
1603-1714

GEORGIAN
1714-
1837

VICTORIAN
1837-1901

MODERN
TIMES
1902-NOW

The Guildhall

> The Corporation bought the Guildhall for about £25 – it was a lot of money in 1548!

The Guildhall used to belong to one of Leicester's religious guilds, and it was closed down by Henry VIII. The town council, known as the Corporation, bought the Guildhall for council meetings, entertainment and even to store coal to sell to the poor. Some say that William Shakespeare performed there.

The Guildhall was used as a town hall until 1876. It is now a museum and performance venue.

SPOT THIS!

If you stand with your back to the fountain in Town Hall Square, you should spot a Tudor Rose. How many more Tudor Roses can you find around Leicester?

Queen Elizabeth I granted Leicester a crest with the Tudor Rose and the motto Semper Eadem ('always the same') on it.

Murder of a Queen

Lady Jane Grey was cousin to King Edward VI – Henry VIII's only son – and it is said that she spent a lonely childhood at her home in Bradgate Park. After Henry and then Edward's deaths, their descendants argued about whether England should be Catholic or Protestant. Lady Jane's Protestant family had her crowned queen in 1553 when she was only 17.

But Henry's eldest daughter, Mary, was Catholic, and insisted that she should be queen. She had Jane beheaded in the Tower of London. Jane's servants were so horrified that some say they cut off the tops of the oak trees in Bradgate Park. There are some trees in the park that look as if they have been beheaded but no one knows if this story is true.

The ruins of Bradgate House can still be seen in Bradgate Park.

CELT
500 BC

ROMAN
AD 43-410

ANGLO-
SAXON
AD 450-
1066

VIKING
AD 865-
1066

MEDIE
TIME
106(
148

The Free Grammar School for boys opened in 1536 and was refounded in 1564, when Queen Elizabeth I began yearly donations of £10 towards the wages of the school's master. This is an imaginary account from Walter – one of the school's pupils.

In 1542, Henry VIII passed a law that all boys must learn Latin using Lily's Latin Grammar Book.

Which is worse? Being beaten with a birch branch or clearing up horse poo?!

Free Grammar School

I am a pupil at the Free Grammar School in St Peter's Church. The building is very old, but Master said that soon we will be moving to a new building in High Cross Street.

We have to be in school for six o'clock every morning, except in winter when we are allowed to go half an hour later. We work until five o'clock in the afternoon with one hour for our midday meal.

We have exams twice a year and they are very hard. There are two Ushers at our school. One of the Ushers is our teacher. He teaches us Latin from Lily's Latin Grammar Book and we practise reading using our horn book. We have to go to church every Sunday.

When we are older we will be in the upper form and the Master will teach us. Then we will have to speak Latin all day. The older boys tell us how hard it is to speak Latin all the time. If they forget, they are beaten with the birch.

Father says that I am lucky. Most boys of my age have to work, like the boy who cleans out Father's horses at the back of our house. But at least he does not have to speak Latin!

The word for horse in Latin is 'equus'. The stable boy might not be educated, but I am!

In 2005, archaeologists began to dig on a site next to the Free Grammar School in High Cross Street, which was built in 1573. They found the remains of Medieval homes and gardens.

TUDOR
1485-
1603

STUART
1603-1714

GEORGIAN
1714-
1837

VICTORIAN
1837-1901

MODERN
TIMES
1902-NOW

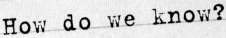

How do we know?

The Leicester Corporation was in charge of the new Free Grammar School, and they wrote reports and letters about the running of the school. There are also written records of meetings at the Guildhall.

However, we do not know very much about life in Tudor Leicester. One reason for this could be because a lot of the records would have been written by monks. These records may well have been destroyed when the Abbey and other religious houses were closed down. The king's men smashed up beautiful works of art. We will never know what treasures were destroyed.

A man called John Leland worked for Henry VIII, travelling around the country making notes about what was happening in different towns. He came to Leicester just before the monasteries were closed, but he did not write things down until many years later. For this reason we cannot be sure that what he wrote is completely true. He may have forgotten things or written what he thought Henry VIII wanted to hear.

There was a huge divide between rich and poor in Tudor Leicester.

A horn book was a piece of parchment stuck to a wooden board with a handle and covered with a thin plate of horn. It was used by schoolchildren to practise their alphabet.

This illustration from 1616 shows a girl from a wealthy family holding a horn book. Girls from poorer homes were only educated in things like sewing, music and obedience!

15

CELT
500 BC

ROMAN
AD 43-410

ANGLO-
SAXON
AD 450-
1066

VIKING
AD 865-
1066

MEDIE
TIME
106(
148

Leicester at War

Robert and his sister watch the wind sending streaks of smoke across the sky from a burning windmill. In the distance, the king's brightly coloured war flags flap as the army approaches. The children are scared. Their father has joined Lord Grey's men and will fight to defend Leicester against the king's army.

Civil War

King Charles I was constantly arguing with Parliament, especially about money and religion. Charles insisted that, because he was the king, he was always right. He refused to let Parliament meet for 11 years.

Lord Thomas Grey, a descendant of Lady Jane Grey, was a Puritan (an extreme Protestant) and Member of Parliament for Leicester. He did not like what the king was doing.

In 1645, during the Civil War, when the Royalist Prince Rupert demanded £2,000 from Leicester, it made the Leicester people hate the king even more. Lord Grey and his men strengthened the Newarke, near the old castle, with ditches and mounds of earth, ready to fight the Royalists.

Charles I was Prince Rupert's uncle. →

Newarke Houses were built in the 1500s. It was here, in the fortified grounds of these buildings, that the Parliamentarians took on the Royalists in 1645. The houses are now a museum.

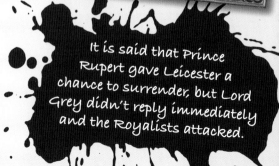

It is said that Prince Rupert gave Leicester a chance to surrender, but Lord Grey didn't reply immediately and the Royalists attacked.

...1625 CHARLES I BECOMES KING...1642 ENGLISH CIVIL WAR BREAKS OUT...

TUDOR
1485–1603

STUART
1603–1714

GEORGIAN
1714–1837

VICTORIAN
1837–1901

MODERN
TIMES
1902–NOW

Siege of Leicester

King Charles, Prince Rupert and the Royalist army camped overnight in St Mary's Fields just outside Leicester. The next morning, on 31st May, 1645, the Royalists charged on the Newarke. The people of Leicester fought hard to defend their town, but Lord Grey's men became surrounded by Royalists in St Martin's Church (now the Cathedral). The Royalists rode through Leicester smashing up property. Over 700 soldiers died.

Two weeks later, however, Charles had lost the war. The victorious Parliamentarians gave Leicester money to repair all the damage. There was enough money left to buy corn and create jobs for the poor.

There has been a church on the site of Leicester Cathedral for over 1,000 years.

Even after the king's men broke through the city walls, the people continued to fight. This is an imaginary diary extract from a young girl called Isabel, who lived in the town.

King Charles was angry that we didn't surrender sooner, but we Leicester folk are brave!

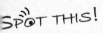
Look closely at the Newarke Houses garden wall and you will see the gun holes punched out by Leicester's soldiers so they could defend the town against the Royalists.

31st May, 1645

Dear Diary,

Yesterday we helped Mother and Aunt Mary fight the King's soldiers. I was so frightened! Cannon fire and musket shots screamed over our heads. We helped to push woolsacks into gaps where cannons had shot holes in the old castle wall. Then we huddled together as musket shots smashed into the wall and splinters of stone showered down on us. Aunt Mary climbed on to the roof of a house with some other ladies. They ripped off slates and, when Prince Rupert's army broke through, they threw the slates – but they could not stop the soldiers.

Stocking Weavers

The sun is setting, and the cottage is getting dark. Ann can hardly see the tiny hooks of yarn that she must thread onto the needles. Her fingers are sore, but she has to help her parents finish the stockings or the truck master will not pay them. Ann's eyes keep closing. She has been working for 15 hours.

Poor Hosiery Workers

In Georgian times, many poor Leicester families had huge stocking frames in their homes. They were heavy to use. Father worked the frame, while mother and children helped with jobs like spinning the thread and hooking up the needles. There were only oil lamps to light the rooms, so families would work in dark conditions. Sometimes, children as young as three were forced to work. Most stocking frames were owned by truck masters, and they charged rent for the machines. They often did not pay the workers with money, but with vouchers that could be used only at shops owned by the truck masters. They were not nice people to work for!

Rich Hosiery Workers

Some people made a lot of money out of hosiery (socks and stockings). They built fine houses and created the beautiful New Walk as a route to the racecourse, which used to be on Victoria Park. Belgrave Hall was built by a rich hosiery merchant. It soon became the centre of a busy hosiery business, paying stockingers who worked in their cottages. The owners of the Hall were good to their workers.

The stocking frame – a mechanical knitting machine – was invented in 1589. It revolutionized the textiles industry.

By 1844, there were more than 18,000 stocking frames in use in Leicester.

...1785 WORK BEGINS ON LEICESTER NAVIGATION CANAL...

Transport Revolution

Coal from the Leicestershire pits was originally transported into town by packhorse. It came through Aylestone, over Packhorse Bridge and along Coal Pit Lane (Braunstone Lane East). In 1785, work began on a canal called the Leicester Navigation. It went from Loughborough to Leicester's West Bridge.

In 1793, hosiery owners paid for a second canal from Market Harborough to Leicester to help carry their heavy goods further afield. It was called the Union Canal.

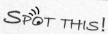 SPOT THIS!

How do you take a boat up a hill? In Leicester, they built Foxton Locks – a big, watery staircase (the largest staircase lock system in the UK). How many locks can you spot?

Packhorse Bridge in Aylestone was built in the 15th century to provide a trade route over swampy ground. It was built specially for horses carrying panniers, so it is narrow with low sides.

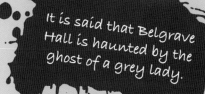

It is said that Belgrave Hall is haunted by the ghost of a grey lady.

In the 18th and 19th centuries hosiery, textiles and shoemaking became Leicester's main industries.

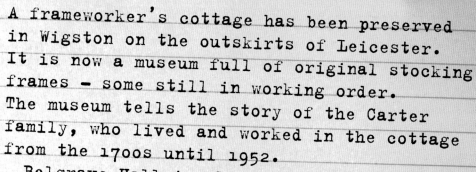

How do we know?

A frameworker's cottage has been preserved in Wigston on the outskirts of Leicester. It is now a museum full of original stocking frames – some still in working order. The museum tells the story of the Carter family, who lived and worked in the cottage from the 1700s until 1952.

Belgrave Hall is also now a museum. The building has been changed over the years, but it has the original fireplace and family crest in the entrance hall.

Foxton Locks Museum near Market Harborough is full of information about Leicester's canals.

Industry Arrives

It is 10 o'clock and the sun is already hot. William pushes through the cheering crowds outside West Bridge Station. He tightly clasps his hard-earned threepence so that pickpockets cannot steal it. A screaming whistle makes him laugh. Clouds of grey-yellow smoke sting his eyes. *The Comet*, Leicester's first steam train, begins its trip through Glenfield Tunnel. What a sight!

When Glenfield Tunnel was built, at over 1,640 metres long, it was the world's longest railway tunnel.

Leicester's New Railway

Leicester's canals could no longer manage to carry all the goods to and from the factories. Leicester needed a railway. John Ellis and several other local businessmen arranged a meeting with the famous engineer George Stephenson. George's son, Robert, became chief engineer and work began. Everyone was very excited. The first engine – *The Comet* – arrived in Leicester on a canal boat and, in 1832, the new railway line opened. Nine years later, Thomas Cook organized the first ever holiday tour – a train trip from Leicester to Loughborough and back.

Tell you what – pot of stewed eels, and you'r free to go!

Industrial Leicester

By the mid-1800s, lots of people were moving to Leicester to work in the new factories – but life was hard. Families were squashed into single rooms with no running water or toilets. Waste ran down the middle of the road. It's not surprising that, in 1849, many Leicester people died of cholera.

The streets were dangerous. There were pickpockets and thieves, and no proper police officers – only a ward constable and a night watchman. They were not paid a wage, so were easily tempted with bribes.

Town Improvements

Leicester became one of the first towns in England to have a proper water supply. New houses were built for the workers in areas such as Highfields and Stoneygate. A proper Borough Police Force was set up and new cells were built under the old Guildhall. Abbey Pumping Station, with its beautifully decorated beam steam engines, was opened. This meant that sewage could be pumped away safely. The pumping engines still work and the regular 'steam-days' are fun to visit.

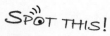 SPOT THIS!

Next time you're walking along London Road near the railway station, look out for this statue of Thomas Cook. His first overseas tour set off from Leicester to Calais in France in 1850.

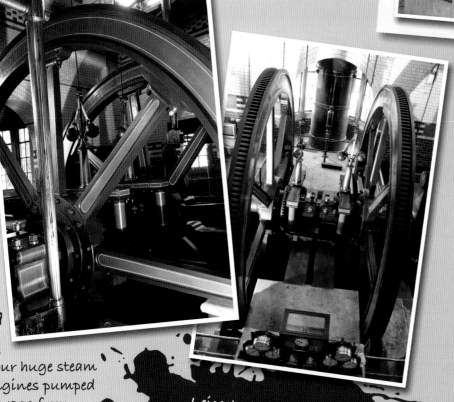

Four huge steam engines pumped sewage from the town to the treatment works at Beaumont Leys.

Leicester's Comet steam engine was the first locomotive to be fitted with a piercing whistle. The whistle was steam-powered, and much louder and more effective than the horns and trumpets used on earlier trains.

In 1840, Tanky Smith became Leicester's first private detective. He was a master of disguise. Can you find the row of heads showing Tanky's many faces? (Look up as you go past the shops near University Road on London Road.)

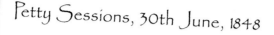

In the 19th century, Leicester's Guildhall was a base for the town's police force and a court and prison for local criminals. This imaginary account is written by a 10-year-old Victorian boy called John. His father is a policeman, and he has taken John to court for the day.

The House of Correction sounds like a horrid place, but I suppose it's better than the cells here – they're spooky!

Petty Sessions, 30th June, 1848

Today, Father let me go to work with him to watch the court at the Guildhall. He said it would teach me how wicked the criminal classes are. I thought the poor people looked hungry, and I said to Father that if they had a job they might not need to steal.

"Nonsense!" said Father. "They are lazy."

The prosecutor and judge sat on a platform at the end of the Great Hall. William Castings, aged 13, was accused of stealing 'one pound weight of butter of the value of one shilling'. The judge sentenced him to a month's hard labour at the House of Correction. The crowd started yelling insults at the boy. I felt sorry for him. I asked Father what the House of Correction is.

"It's the new gaol on Welford Road where he'll be shown what real work is," said Father.

Next, a thin boy was brought into the Great Hall. His clothes were ripped and dirty. He was only a year older than me. I felt sad when the judge said,

"This Court finds Michael Hansbury, aged 11 years, guilty of stealing three buns of the value of one penny."

I wonder what will happen to him.

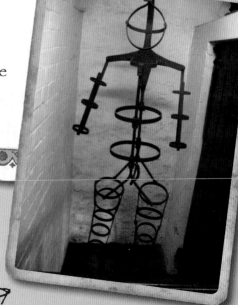

The Guildhall is said to be Leicester's most haunted building – watch out for the ghosts of Victorian policemen and a mysterious 'White Lady'!

This gibbet hangs in one of the cells. It was used to display the bodies of criminals to deter others from a life of crime.

How do we know?

The Guildhall was used as a courtroom for centuries. Records of the Petty Sessions from that time, along with the case notes of William Casting and Michael Hansbury, are in the Wigston Records Office.

The Guildhall is still used today, but not as a court. You can visit the cells and meet 'Crankie Gemmie' and 'Emma Smith' – two of Leicester's notorious Victorian pickpockets.

Victorian newspapers were not very exciting to read, and few people could read anyway, but they mean we have a record of lots of things that happened in Victorian Leicester – such as the opening of the railways shown below. John Ellis was a councillor, Midland Railway Company Chairman and MP, so we have plenty of written evidence to tell us about his work.

We also know what a lot of the buildings and streets looked like in Leicester in the 1800s because artist John Flower sketched them in his book 'Views of Ancient Buildings in the Town and County of Leicester' published in 1826.

> Leicester's population grew, and the town became a safer, healthier place to live.

John Flower painted West Bridge (left) in 1826 and High Cross (below) in 1830. They give us a snapshot of life in Leicester in the 19th century.

The Leicester Journal, 20th July, 1832

"The Leicester and Swannington Railway was opened on Tuesday last, the day being ushered in with ringing of bells, firing of cannon and other demonstrations of joy... the whole engine advanced at a very rapid pace... and soon arrived at the entrance of the tunnel. It is impossible to conceive the feeling... on exchanging the glaring light of a July sun for the almost impenetrable darkness of this subterranean passage..."

Home From Home

It's November 1972. The sky is grey. At home it was always blue. Shanti waves goodbye as his mother leaves for her first day of work in Leicester. Two weeks ago they were forced to leave their home in Uganda. They were allowed to take only £50 and the clothes they could carry. Now Shanti shivers in a strange, cold town – his new home.

Corah started as a small family business. Nathaniel Corah bought items of clothing from locals at the Globe Inn every Saturday, then took them to his warehouse in Birmingham.

Jobs in Leicester

There were many jobs in Leicester in the boot and shoe industry, and also in engineering. Sir Frank Whittle developed the jet engine in an engineering factory just outside the city. The only problem was that his factory was close to houses, and the local people complained about the noise. The hosiery industry still provided lots of jobs for Leicester's workers into the 1970s. One of the big factories was called Corah, and it made clothes for Marks & Spencer.

Look out for the Frank Whittle memorial in the middle of a roundabout outside Lutterworth.

TUDOR
1485-1603

STUART
1603-1714

GEORGIAN
1714-1837

VICTORIAN
1837-1901

MODERN
TIMES
1902-NOW

New Arrivals

Many different groups of people have settled in Leicester since 1930. During World War Two few bombs fell on Leicester, and a lot of families were evacuated to the city to escape the terrible bombing in London. Many of them decided to stay on after the war.

It is impossible to list all the groups of people who have arrived in Leicester since the end of World War Two, but here are a few of them:

The first black immigrants arrived from the Caribbean shortly after the war. They came to Leicester because the town needed extra workers. The factories were so busy and so many men had been away fighting in the war that there was a shortage of workers.

When India and Pakistan were divided into two countries in 1947 many people from the borders were not happy. They heard that there were jobs in Leicester, and moved into the Spinney Hill and Belgrave areas.

Leicester University's Attenborough Building was named after naturalist and presenter Sir David Attenborough's father, Frederick, who was principal of the University. David and his actor brother Lord Richard Attenborough both went to Wyggeston Grammar School as boys.

SPOT THIS!

The first official Jain temple in the western world was in Leicester. Take a look at this beautiful building next time you're in Oxford Street. How many pillars can you spot?

In 1948, the ship MV Empire Windrush brought 492 immigrants from the West Indies to England.

In 1972, the Ugandan leader Idi Amin ordered all Asians to leave Uganda. They had to leave very quickly and were not allowed to bring all their belongings with them. More than 20,000 Ugandan Asians arrived in Leicester.

In the 1990s, both Kosovan and Somali refugees escaped to Leicester from wars where they would have been killed or tortured had they stayed. People also came from Montserrat after a volcanic eruption meant that it was not safe to stay in their homes.

Many other groups of people have settled in Leicester, including Chinese, Polish and Irish – turning the city into the multi-ethnic, multi-cultural community that it is today.

CELT
500 BC

ROMAN
AD 43-410

ANGLO-
SAXON
AD 450-
1066

VIKING
AD 865-
1066

MEDIE
TIMI
106
148

Life was not always easy for immigrants from other countries trying to settle and make a home in Leicester. Many immigrants found it hard to get used to the different climate, language and diet. In this imaginary account, a Pakistani boy called Amit talks about his new life in Leicester.

By the year 2012, ethnic groups will make up the majority of the population of Leicester.

It is 1960 and we've been in Leicester for three years. My name is Amit and I'm learning English at school, but my parents can only speak Gujarati. They would like to learn English but there is no one here who can teach them. I teach them what I can, though. There are not any shops here where we can buy the food that we used to eat at home, but my father knows a man who will deliver lentils and other food to our house. When we first arrived we couldn't even get yogurt - people in Leicester don't like it! But a local dairy has started to make it for us.

Everybody in Leicester is friendly, even though sometimes they do not understand what we are saying. There is no gurdwara for us to pray in, but we are allowed to use a room at the school. Every weekend we go to Spinney Hill Park and I play with my little sister Navrita while my father talks with his friends. Sometimes there is an Asian film at the local cinema and we all go. That is really exciting because we have fun together and feel at home.

Mum! Dad! Come and sit down - it's time for you to do your English homework!

Spinney Hill Park was created by Leicester City Corporation in the 1880s to provide the growing population with open space to exercise and play in. The fountain in the park was donated in 1888 by wealthy local pork and cheese merchant and councillor Samuel Mather.

| TUDOR 1485-1603 | STUART 1603-1714 | GEORGIAN 1714-1837 | VICTORIAN 1837-1901 | MODERN TIMES 1902-NOW |

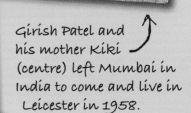

Girish Patel and his mother Kiki (centre) left Mumbai in India to come and live in Leicester in 1958.

How do we know?

We know what it was like for Gujarati families like Amit's, who arrived in Leicester in 1957, because the Oral History Society at Leicester University has collected interviews from people who have lots of different memories of Leicester at that time.

The main way that Leicester people find out about what has been happening in their city, especially since the 1930s, is by reading the local newspapers. The Leicester Mercury has been Leicester's main local newspaper for more than 100 years. There was also the Leicester Chronicle and the Leicester Journal. You can look at old copies of all these newspapers at the Records Office in Wigston.

National newspapers, television and radio reports, especially Radio Leicester, have made sure that we know about issues in Leicester and are aware of the problems of some people abroad who are being tortured and driven out of their countries.

Leicester has become a multi-cultural city. For 45% of primary school children, English is a second language.

27

CELT
500 BC

ROMAN
AD 43-410

ANGLO-
SAXON
AD 450-
1066

VIKING
AD 865-
1066

MEDIE
TIM
106
148

Leicester Today and Tomorrow...

It is the first Saturday in August. The sun is blazing down on Victoria Park. Tracey and Farhana are dressed in butterfly outfits ready for the carnival procession to move off down London Road. After the procession they will come back to the park, eat sticks of sugar cane and dance to the music.

The Walkers Stadium in Filbert Way is Leicester City FC's ground. The stadium seats 32,500 fans, and was opened by Gary Lineker in 2002.

There has been a Caribbean carnival in Leicester since 1985. It is the largest UK Caribbean carnival apart from the one at Notting Hill in London.

Belgrave Road is filled with the fabulous aroma of Indian restaurants. It is glittering with brightly coloured sari shops and Indian jewellers. During Diwali people visit from all over the country to see the amazing lights and join in with the celebrations, which include lots of food and fireworks.

A quarter of a million people visit the Space Centre every year. A glass lift takes you up to the 42 metre high Rocket Tower. You can go on a 3D mission through the Solar System, land on the moon and pilot The Eagle onto the lunar surface. Far out!

...1983 FIRST DIWALI STREET LIGHTS...1985 FIRST CARIBBEAN CARNIVAL...

Leicester is home to the biggest covered outdoor market in Europe – and it has been on the same site since Viking times. The market is still protected by a royal charter issued 700 years ago that forbids other markets from opening nearby.

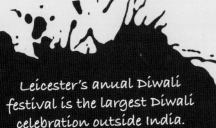

Leicester's anual Diwali festival is the largest Diwali celebration outside India.

SPOT THIS!

The Clock Tower was built in 1868 on a site that used to be a hay and straw market outside the old town. It is now in the centre of town. The tower has four statues of the 'sons of Leicester' – one on each corner. William Wyggeston is one. Who are the other three?

Leicester has changed a lot since it was called Ratae Corieltauvorum... or has it? The new High Cross shopping centre is close to the site of the Anglo-Saxon market.

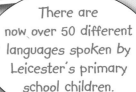

There are now over 50 different languages spoken by Leicester's primary school children.

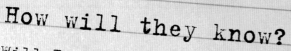

How will they know?

Will Leicester always look like it does today? How will future generations know what Leicester was like today? The Internet is a great way of recording events. Photos, blogs and stories from tourists can all spread the word about our wonderful city. Or maybe you'll be famous one day and put Leicester on the map!

Glossary

Abbey – a Christian monastery or convent, run by an abbott.

AD – a short way of writing the Latin words anno Domini, which mean 'in the year of our Lord', i.e. after the birth of Christ.

Archaeologist – a person who studies the past by looking at the remains left behind by people and cultures.

Artefact – another word for an object, often an archaeological one.

Atrium – the main court of a Roman house.

BC – a short way of writing 'before the birth of Christ'.

Catholic – a member of the Christian religion that considers the pope to be the head of its church.

Cholera – a deadly disease caused by drinking dirty water.

Christianity – a religion based on the life and teachings of Jesus of Nazareth.

Evacuate – to leave home and live somewhere else for safety, often because of war.

Fort – a strong building offering support and protection.

Forum – a meeting place used to discuss things in public.

Gladiator – a man trained to fight in an arena for entertainment in Roman times.

Gurdwara – a place of worship for Sikhs.

Hosiery – socks, stockings, and tights.

Immigrant – a person who comes from a foreign country in order to settle here.

Jain temple – a place of worship for people of the Jain religion.

Latin – a language originally spoken in Ancient Rome.

Mosaic – a design or decoration made up of small pieces of coloured glass or stone.

Motte and bailey castle – a form of castle built on a raised mound of earth and surrounded by a fence.

Packhorse – a horse used to carry goods on its back.

Parliamentarian – also known as a Roundhead: anyone who fought on the side of Parliament against Charles I in the English Civil War.

Pickpocket – a thief who steals from the pockets or purses of others.

Plague – a serious disease that is carried by rats and can be transferred to humans by fleas.

Protestant – a member of the Christian religion that considers the king or queen to be the head of its church.

Refugee – a person who flees to another country because they no longer feel safe in their own country.

Royal charter – written permission from the king or queen to do something.

Royalist – anyone who fought on the side of King Charles I in the English Civil War.

Slave – any person who is owned by another. Slaves have no freedom or rights and work for no payment.

Truck master – a man who owned and rented out stocking frames for hosiery workers to use in Georgian Leicester.

Wattle and daub – a method of building houses using sticks covered in mud and animal dung.

Index

Acknowledgements

The publishers would like to thank the following people and organizations
for their permission to reproduce material on the following pages:
p5: Jewry Wall Museum; p6: Jewry Wall Museum; p7: Jewry Wall Museum; p9: Jewry Wall Museum;
p13: John Bennett; p14: University of Leicester Archaeological Services; p15: Phrood/Wikipedia;
p19: Burn the asylum/Wikipedia; p20: MaltaGC/Wikipedia; p21: Leicester Pumping Station;
p22: Richard Chaplin/flikr; p23: Shadygrove2007/Wikipedia; p25: Illustrated London News Ltd/Mary Evans;
p26: Kate Jewel/geograph, Mat Fascione/geograph; p27: Belgrave Memories, EMEN www.emen.org.uk;
p28: WalkerStadium-Bot, Magnus Manske-wikipedia

Written by Rosalind Adam
Educational consultant: Neil Thompson
Local history consultant: Richard Buckley
Designed by Stephen Prosser

Illustrated by Kate Davies, Dynamo Limited, Peter Kent,
John MacGregor, Leighton Noyes and Tim Sutcliffe.
Additional photographs by Alex Long

First published by HOMETOWN WORLD in 2011
Hometown World Ltd
7 Northumberland Buildings
Bath BA1 2JB

www.hometownworld.co.uk

hb ISBN 978-1-84993-128-1
pb ISBN 978-1-84993-149-6

CELT	ROMAN	ANGLO-SAXON	VIKING	MEDIEVAL TIME
500 BC	AD 43-410	AD 450-1066	AD 865-1066	1066-1485